Profiles in Greek and Roman Mythology

ARTEMIS

P.O. Box 196
Hockessin, Delaware 19707
Visit us on the web: www.mitchelllane.com
Comments? email us: mitchelllane@mitchelllane.com

PROFILES IN GREEK AND ROMAN MYTHOLOGY

Titles in the Series

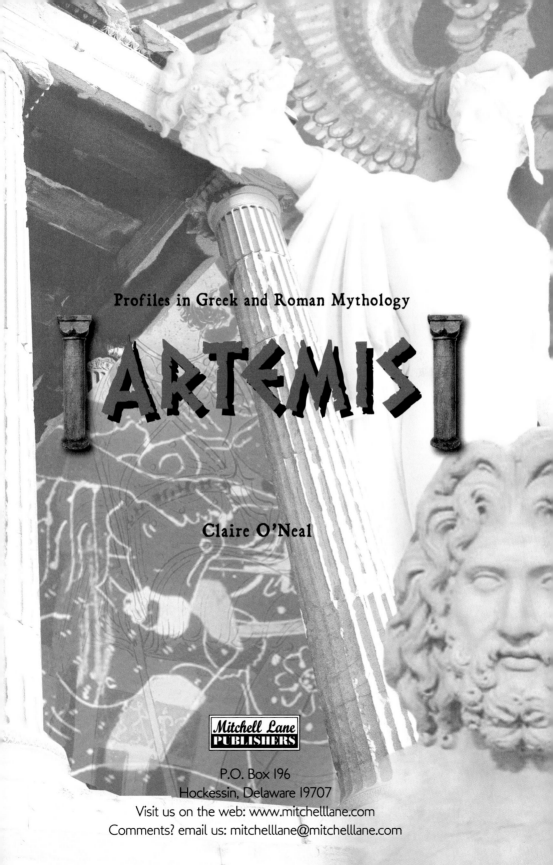

Profiles in Greek and Roman Mythology

ARTEMIS

Claire O'Neal

Mitchell Lane
PUBLISHERS

P.O. Box 196
Hockessin, Delaware 19707
Visit us on the web: www.mitchelllane.com
Comments? email us: mitchelllane@mitchelllane.com

Printing   2   3   4   5   6   7   8   9

Library of Congress Cataloging-in-Publication Data

O'Neal, Claire.
  Artemis / by Claire O'Neal.
      p. cm. — (Profiles in Greek and Roman mythology)
  Includes bibliographical references and index.
  ISBN 978-1-58415-555-3 (library bound)
  1. Artemis (Greek deity)—Juvenile literature. I. Title.
  BL820.D5O54 2007
  398.20938'01—dc22
                                                              2007023485

ABOUT THE AUTHOR: Claire O'Neal became hooked on mythology in the fourth grade,
when she read a collection of Greek myths she found in her school library. Spurred on to
read nearly everything in her path, she has earned degrees in English literature, biology, and
chemistry, and has published both poetry and scientific research. She lives in Delaware with her
husband, two young boys, and a big black cat. This is her first book for Mitchell Lane Publishers.

PHOTO CREDITS: pp. 6, 8—Barbara Marvis; p. 11—Jastrow; p. 14—Jonathan Scott; p. 16—
Bloemaert; p. 17—Timanthus; p. 21—JupiterImages; p. 22—Peter Paul Rubens; p. 24—Harry and
Margaret P. Glicksman Endowment Fund purchase; p. 28—National Gallery of Scotland; p. 30—
Jean-Baptiste Lemoyne; p. 33—University of Oklahoma; p. 36—Marcobadotti; p. 38—Nicolas
Poussin; p. 41—The University of Georgia

PUBLISHER'S NOTE: This story is based on the author's extensive research, which she
believes to be accurate. Documentation of such research is contained on page 45. Portions of
this story have been retold using dialogue as an aid to readability. The dialogue is based on the
author's research and approximates what might have occurred at the time. The internet sites
referenced herein were active as of the publication date. Due to the fleeting nature of some web
sites, we cannot guarantee they will all be active when you are reading this book.
     To reflect current usage, we have chosen to use the secular era designations BCE
("before the common era") and CE ("of the common era") instead of the traditional
designations BC ("before Christ") and AD (*anno Domini*, "in the year of the Lord").

PLB, PLB4

TABLE OF CONTENTS

Profiles in Greek and Roman Mythology

The Greek goddess Artemis looks to the right and, spotting her prey, reaches to draw an arrow from the quiver slung over her right shoulder. In the first or second century CE, Roman sculptors copied this famous marble statue, *Artemis the Huntress*, from a bronze version, now lost, which was sculpted by the Athenian Leochares in 325 BCE. Leochares also put his talents to work on the walls of the Mausoleum of Mausolus, one of the Seven Wonders of the Ancient World.

The Virgin Goddess
and Her Sacred Deer

One day a young prince named Actaeon (AK-tee-on) and his friends went to the woods around Mount Cithaeron (SIH-thuh-ron) to hunt deer. As the sun began to set, the party grew tired and headed home. Actaeon wanted to explore the woods on his way, perhaps to find untouched hunting grounds, and took a different path home alone.

Artemis (AR-tuh-mis), the virgin goddess of the hunt, had been hunting with her nymphs in the same mountains, and she too was weary. As she headed back to her home with the other gods on Mount Olympus (oh-LIM-pus), she passed one of her favorite spots— a natural pool near a cave enclosed by a grove of cypress trees. "How lovely it would be to end the day with a bath," thought Artemis. She stopped at the pool and undressed, washing her long, white limbs in the clear waters while her nymphs swam around her or relaxed at the pool's edge.

Actaeon had wandered nearby and heard the unusual sound of girls talking and splashing. Following the peal of their laughter, he soon entered a grove he hadn't seen before. "What are so many women doing here in the middle of the woods, away from their homes?" he wondered. When curious Actaeon hid behind a tree trunk for an innocent look, he saw what no man's eyes had ever seen before—the goddess Artemis, naked. Actaeon knew he should have turned away and continued on to meet his friends, but instead he secretly watched the goddess. He had never seen anything so beautiful and, as he stared at her, he knew he was falling in love.

It wasn't long before Artemis' nymphs spotted Actaeon. Surprised, they jumped up and tried to block his view, forming a circle around her with their bodies and shouting in a deafening roar. The nymphs

In Greek art, Artemis was a hunter in action. She was often shown in the act of shooting and wore her tunic short so it wouldn't slow her down. An animal such as a hunting dog or, in *Artemis the Huntress*, a stag, accompanied her. Her left hand grips the handle of a bow now lost from the statue.

couldn't do much to hide Artemis' face, as the goddess stood a whole head taller than her protectors. Artemis looked the hunter straight in the eye and blushed—she knew he had seen her bathing.

Angry Artemis looked for her bow and arrow in their usual place at her side, but she had left them on the bank. Reaching for the only potential weapon at hand, she scooped a handful of water and flung it at him, saying, "Now you may tell, if you can tell that is, of having seen me naked!"[1] The cursed droplets hit poor Actaeon and turned him into a deer. Frightened, he galloped away through the woods. He tried calling to his hunting party for help but no sound came from his mouth.

Actaeon's friends were quite near. As Actaeon crossed their path, the hunters did not recognize their prince, but instead saw the most magnificent deer yet. They sent Actaeon's own dogs after him. Actaeon ran as he tried to calm the dogs, saying, "I am Actaeon!

Know your own master!" but again the words didn't come. At last, the dogs caught him and ripped their teeth into his soft skin. His friends laughed with each other at how Actaeon would have loved to see his hounds wrestling with such a prize animal, not knowing that their friend was there all along, dying right before their eyes.

Ancient Greek Religion

The story of the ill-fated Actaeon is a myth—meaning "story," "word," or even "speech"—told by ancient Greeks to describe the gods and goddesses of their religion. Greek religion was based upon many myths that sought to explain the mysteries of nature and life. In myth, gods had supernatural powers that caused natural events such as a sunrise or an earthquake. Gods also ruled the human body and mind. They were responsible for birth and death and for human emotions, especially love. Ancient Greek religion is no longer practiced, but people can study it today because the writings of its practitioners survive, and the myths continue to influence Western thought and culture. Myths also give us an opportunity to understand the culture and values of ancient Greece.

No single book exists that records every Greek myth, because myths were developed piecemeal over a long period of time. Before Greek writing evolved in the eighth century BCE, myths were passed along through storytellers. Starting in the 700s BCE, the great Greek poet Homer wrote down some of the most influential stories. Other writers followed, each usually telling a myth a little differently. This variety sometimes complicated the stories, but the plots and major characters stayed mostly the same, giving all Greeks a communal knowledge of important myths.

There are literally hundreds of characters in Greek mythology, but most myths involve one or more of the twelve Olympians. These most powerful gods and goddesses were so called because they were thought to live atop Mount Olympus, the highest mountain in Greece. The Actaeon myth tells us about the goddess Artemis, a

major player in the Greek pantheon. She is the virgin goddess of the hunt, the wilderness, and childbirth. In addition to Artemis, the Olympians were Zeus (ZOOS), the king of the gods; Hera (HAYR-uh) goddess of marriage; Poseidon (poh-SY-dun), god of the sea; Hades (HAY-deez), god of the dead and the underworld; Hermes (HUR-meez), the messenger god; Athena (uh-THEE-nuh), goddess of civilization; Aphrodite (aa-froh-DY-tee), goddess of love; Hephaestus (huh-FES-stus), god of technology; Ares (AIR-eez), god of war; Demeter (DIH-mih-ter), goddess of farming and agriculture; and Apollo (ah-PAH-loh), god of medicine and truth.

To a modern audience, Greek myths seem like a sort of ancient soap opera. The gods and goddesses fought with each other, fell in and out of love, and, most importantly, interfered in the lives of mortals.

The Ceryneian Hind

One of the most famous of these mortals was Heracles (HAYR-uh-kleez), better known by his Roman name, Hercules (HER-kyoo-leez). He was himself a son of Zeus by the mortal woman Alcmene (alk-MEE-nee), and not by Zeus' wife, Hera. One day, jealous Hera set a fit of madness upon Hercules that made him kill his own wife and children. A distraught Hercules consulted the Oracle at Delphi (DEL-fy), who told him that he could only be cleansed of his horrible deed by serving his archenemy Eurystheus (yuh-RISS-thee-us) for twelve years. Eurystheus gave the hero twelve dangerous tasks to perform, hoping to send Hercules to his death. Instead, Hercules completed them all with strength, agility, and cunning.

One task was to capture the Ceryneian (seh-rih-NEE-un) Hind, a deer with golden hooves and horns that roamed Mount Ceryneia in Arcadia. Unlike the beasts that Hercules had conquered before, the deer could not attack him, but neither could Hercules attack it because the beast was sacred to Artemis. The hind was one of five; Artemis had caught the other four deer and they now pulled her

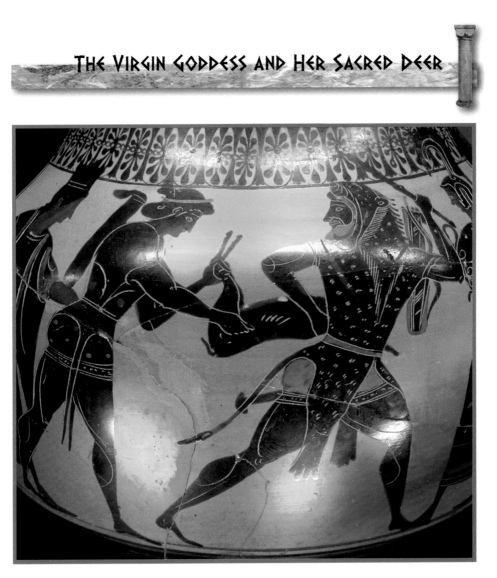

A ceramic amphora, painted between 530 and 520 BCE, show Hercules capturing the Ceryneian Hind. The Greeks used tall, slender amphorae as storage and transport containers for foods and liquids. Wider, beautifully decorated amphorae like this one were used at special events like festivals, weddings, and funerals.

chariot. But Hera caused the Ceryneian Hind to speed away from Artemis and into the mountains, setting up this future labor for Hercules.

Hercules spent a year chasing the swift hind around the mountain. How he finally caught it is disputed. Some sources say he used a net; others say he grabbed it while it slept or stopped for a drink; still others say he landed a perfectly aimed arrow that wounded the deer or pinned its legs together without bloodshed. With his prize captured, Hercules slung the deer over his shoulders and carried it down the mountain. Artemis stopped him before he got too far. She was furious and threatened to punish him for stealing her pet. Hercules begged her for mercy, telling her that he meant no disrespect and that it was all Eurystheus' idea. Artemis took pity on him, and was also secretly impressed that Hercules caught the deer when she could not. She gave Hercules her blessing to take the hind to his master.

The myths of Actaeon and the Ceryneian Hind illustrate Artemis' control over wild animals and hunting, but her character is much more complex than that. She also protects women, especially in childbirth. Her important myths show how easily and thoroughly these different aspects blend together in Artemis. That she can be all these things at once also helps us understand more about the roles of women in ancient Greece.

The largest statue of Artemis is found in the Prytaneion at Ephesus. The statue is 9.5 feet (2.9 meters) high. It dates to the first century CE.

A Modern Artemis

Hercules and Hippolyte, the Amazon queen

Wonder Woman is a comic book heroine created by psychologist William Moulton Marston. The comic is heavily influenced by Greek myth, and especially by Artemis. Wonder Woman was born when Amazon queen Hippolyte (hih-PAH-luh-tee) wished for a daughter to act as a missionary of peace for the Amazon women. The gods heard Hippolyte and told her to sculpt a baby girl out of clay, which they then gave life. Hippolyte named her new daughter Diana (Artemis' Roman name) after the Amazons' favorite goddess.

According to the comic, Diana became known as Wonder Woman when she impressed American culture with her special powers. Though Diana is mortal, she "possesses godlike strength, speed, invulnerability, and the ability to fly."[2] Artemis, like any god, would have had similar abilities. Like Artemis, Wonder Woman is an excellent hunter and can communicate with animals. Unlike Artemis, Wonder Woman is not an archer, but, according to her comic, uses other weapons, including a "magic lasso which compels its captives to speak the truth, a boomerang tiara that can cut through diamond, and bracelets that can deflect gunfire."[3] Also unlike Artemis, Wonder Woman is susceptible to love. Her true love is Steve Trevor, a pilot she met when his plane crash-landed in her homeland.

Marston developed the lie detector test in 1915. While testing the device, he suggested that women lied less frequently than men. He became convinced that women were more honest and good than men and spent his life speaking out for women's rights.

He used comic books to introduce his ideas to a larger audience. When Wonder Woman first appeared in 1941, every comic book hero was male. As Garland Voss puts it, "Like Superman's lady love Lois Lane, comic book women were helpless onlookers never capable of accomplishing the incredible feats of the men who dominated them."[4] The uniqueness of Marston's Wonder Woman scored big with readers, and she has been in press ever since.

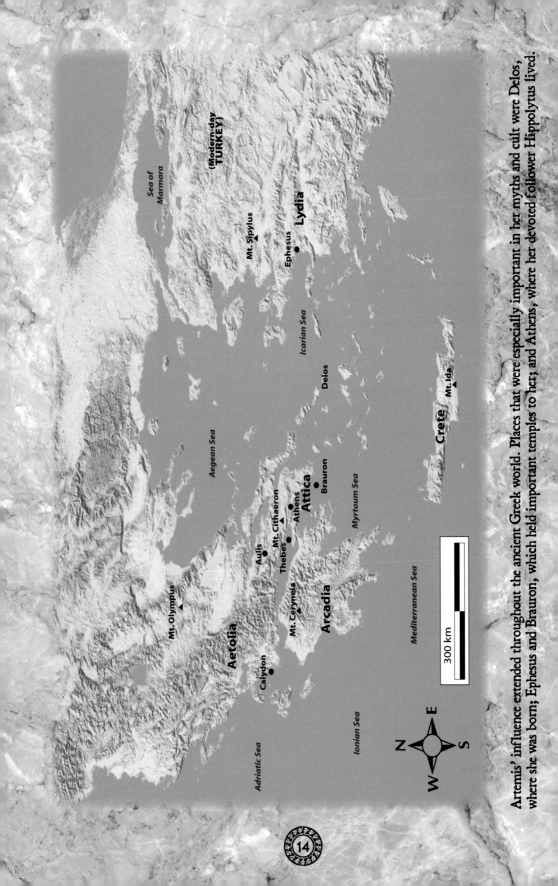

Artemis' influence extended throughout the ancient Greek world. Places that were especially important in her myths and cult were Delos, where she was born; Ephesus and Brauron, which held important temples to her; and Athens, where her devoted follower Hippolytus lived.

CHAPTER 2

Religious with a Vengeance

Because the gods were thought to protect those who properly worshiped them, myths warned that failure to give the gods their due would have disastrous consequences. Artemis was particularly violent when ignored or insulted. As Callimachus put it, "Those on whom the goddess smiles have rich fields, healthy herds, and long life. The unjust, however, on whom the goddess frowns, will suffer. Plague destroys their cattle, frost destroys their fields, and their women either die in childbirth or, if they do survive, give birth to infants unable to stand on upright ankle."[1] Artemis' punishments were always harsh and usually deadly, as seen in the myths of Niobe (ny-OH-bee) and Iphigenia (ih-fih-jih-NY-uh).

Niobe

Niobe was the queen of Thebes, beautiful and fabulously wealthy. She came from a famous family—she was Zeus' granddaughter, and her husband, Amphion (AM-fee-on), was Zeus' son. Niobe was particularly fond of her fourteen children, seven boys and seven girls. But she was also fond of herself and took her good fortune for granted.

One day a seer urged all Theban women to sacrifice to the goddess Leto (LEE-toh). Niobe refused, saying, "Why worship gods you can't see, when I am right in front of you? I count Zeus in my family tree, and my beauty, power, and wealth is known throughout the land. Surely I am more worthy of worship than Leto. What has she done but borne a mere two children?" Niobe also carelessly suggested she could lose a few offspring and still make Leto seem almost childless by comparison. Perhaps she had given the goddess a wicked idea.

From their immortal perch in the clouds, Artemis and Apollo shoot to kill in *The Death of Niobe's Children*, painted by Abraham Bloemaert in 1591.

Leto heard Niobe's arrogant words and called on her faithful children, Apollo and Artemis, to avenge her. They agreed that Niobe's insults could not be tolerated and flew down to Thebes, where first Apollo saw Niobe's sons exercising in the palace courtyard. One by one, he killed them all with his arrows. When Amphion saw this, his grief was so overwhelming, he killed himself with his own sword. Niobe was shocked. Ignoring her former dignity, she covered her sons' bodies with her own, crying and kissing them. Yet instead of learning her lesson, Niobe's sorrow only fueled her anger. She spat at Leto, "Even in my misery I have more than you in your happiness. After so many deaths, I still outdo you!"[2]

At that, it was Artemis' turn. Niobe's daughters rushed out to their fallen brothers, making themselves easy targets. One by one, Artemis shot them with her divine arrows. Only Niobe was left alive, surrounded by her dead family. Her sadness was so great that she stood stunned and unmoving, her face pale as marble. As tears silently streamed from her eyes, her body rigid with horror, she turned to stone. The gods whisked her away to the top of Mount Sipylus, where to this day it is said that a rock in her image still weeps.

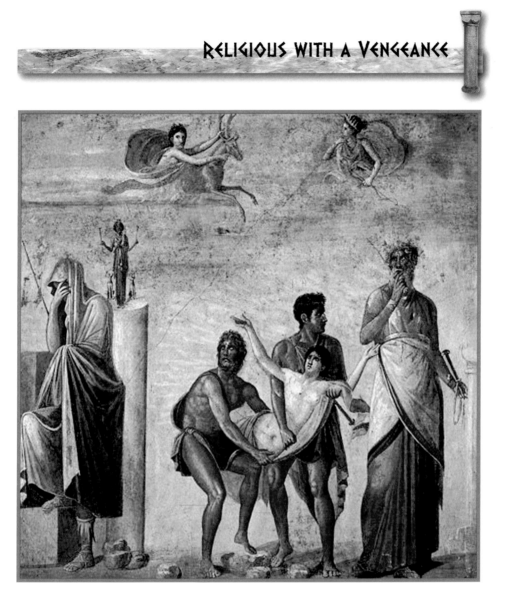

As Iphigenia is carried away, her father, Agamemnon, hides his face. The Greeks considered Agamemnon's plight to be a classic example of grief. The girl does not die in this Roman fresco, *The Sacrifice of Iphigenia*, based on a lost fourth-century BCE painting by Timanthus. A magnificent deer escorts Iphigenia through the sky to a waiting Artemis.

Iphigenia

The Greek navy assembled at Aulis under the command of Agamemnon (aa-guh-MEM-non). A Trojan prince named Paris had kidnapped Helen, the beautiful wife of Agamemnon's brother Menelaus (meh-

nuh-LAY-us). Agamemnon and his fellow Greek commanders were bound by an oath to Helen's father, Tyndareus (tin-DAYR-ee-us), to protect Helen. They hastily prepared to attack Troy and get her back.

As the eager soldiers readied their ships to launch, the wind suddenly and ominously died. The great fleet stood still in the water, their sails empty.

Agamemnon consulted a seer named Calchas (KAL-kus), who told him that this was no ordinary calm. Calchas said, "Artemis is angry at you, Agamemnon, and is holding the winds for ransom." On a recent hunting trip, Agamemnon had not only killed a deer sacred to the goddess, but had also boasted that he was a better hunter than Artemis. Calchas named the goddess's price: "She won't let us leave port until you have sacrificed your prettiest daughter, Iphigenia, at her temple."

Agamemnon loved his daughter dearly and at first refused. But when he saw his restless army, he knew they could revolt and kill her anyway if he didn't get the ships moving soon. He also remembered his oath to Tyndareus. With a heavy heart, he sent for Iphigenia, but asked the messenger to lie and say she was coming to marry the hero Achilles (uh-KIH-leez).

Iphigenia hurried to Aulis, excited by the news, but the first person she met was Achilles. Together they learned the truth. Achilles was furious that his name had been used to trick the girl. He argued with Agamemnon that she should be spared. Iphigenia listened, overhearing her father's reasoning for her sacrifice. She realized that, in death, she performed an important duty for Greece. She bravely accepted her fate, saying, "If Artemis is minded to take this body, am I, a weak mortal, to thwart the goddess?"[3]

They journeyed to the temple to perform the sacrifice—but what happened after Iphigenia climbed atop the altar is disputed. In one version, Agamemnon took the knife and, covering his tear-stained eyes with his hands, slit his own daughter's throat. Other authors say that Iphigenia's willingness to die impressed Artemis, who decided to let her live. In Euripides' play *Iphigenia at Aulis*, just as the priest

Calchas plunges a knife toward Iphigenia's body, Artemis substitutes a deer's carcass for the girl, whisking her away to become a priestess at Tauris. Calchas explains, "This is more welcome to [Artemis] by far than the maid, that she may not defile her altar by shedding noble blood."[4] Either way, Artemis was satisfied and filled the Greek sails with winds blowing toward Troy.

Temples to Artemis

A true example of public worship and sacrifice started with the rich King Croesus (KREE-sus) of Lydia. After conquering the ancient city of Ephesus (in modern-day Turkey) in 550 BCE, he wanted to honor the gods who had blessed him. Croesus commissioned a spectacular marble temple in place of the lowly but long-attended local shrine to Artemis. Pliny the Elder reported that the temple took 120 years to build and was an almost unbelievable size, 220 feet wide and 425 feet long. The Temple of Artemis at Ephesus became known as one of the Seven Wonders of the World. As Antipater of Sidon described: "When I saw the house of Artemis that mounted to the clouds, those other marvels lost their brilliancy, and I said, 'Lo, apart from [Mount] Olympus, the Sun never looked on [anything] so grand.' "[5]

Its fame attracted the attention of a lunatic named Herostratus. He burned the temple to the ground on July 21, 356 BCE, the very day the conqueror Alexander the Great was born. As Plutarch said, "It was no wonder that the temple of Artemis was burned down, since the goddess was busy bringing Alexander into the world."[6] Herostratus hoped his horrific act would put his name in the history books, so after the Ephesians executed him they forbade his name from being written down. Their efforts worked for a time, though eventually Strabo told his tale. In the fourth century BCE, Alexander the Great himself visited Ephesus and offered money to rededicate a new temple. The Ephesians wittily refused, saying, "It is not fitting for one god to dedicate a temple to another."[7] The temple was restored after Alexander's death in 323 BCE. By the time the Romans took over in the second century BCE

and Artemis became known as Diana, the temple was so famous that images of its statues were minted on some Roman coins.

Christianity and the decline of the Roman Empire brought the temple's heyday to an end. The New Testament of the Bible records how local craftsmen, sensing a threat to the temple's commerce, incited riots in Ephesus when Paul preached there: "And when they heard these sayings, they were full of wrath, and cried out, saying, Great is Diana of the Ephesians."[8] When raids closer to home forced Rome to withdraw their military from Ephesus, the temple was sacked by the Goths, a warlike European tribe, in 262 CE. Any hopes that it would be restored were dashed in 391 CE, when emperor Theodosius I declared Christianity the official state religion and shut down government support to the polytheistic temples. After falling into disuse, the temple was destroyed by a mob in 401 CE, and over time, its ruins were buried in silt deposits from the Mediterranean Sea.

In 1869 CE, British archaeologist John Turtle Wood rediscovered the temple under 15 feet of mud. Wood found unusual statues of Artemis with round objects protruding from her chest. Scholars weren't sure if the objects were breasts, eggs, or even bull testicles, but all agreed that the statues depicted a goddess of fertility. This was not exactly unexpected. Greek religion evolved through syncretism, wherein early Greeks incorporated the deities of peoples they conquered into their own gods. This is how Artemis, the virgin goddess of the hunt, also became a goddess of childbirth.

Seven Wonders of the Ancient World

Temple of Artemis at Gerasa (modern-day Jerash in Jordan)

Herodotus, a Greek historian, named seven magnificent structures, built by Mediterranean civilizations, as Wonders of the World. Artemis' Temple at Ephesus is one. The other six are:

Great Pyramid of Giza. A tomb for the Pharaoh Khufu, the Pyramid was built near Cairo, Egypt, around 2560 BCE. Laborers slaved for more than 20 years to place 2 million, two-ton blocks of stone to make the 481-foot-tall structure. The only Wonder still standing, the pyramid inspired an Arab proverb: "Man fears time, but time fears the pyramids."[9]

Hanging Gardens of Babylon. Around 600 BCE, King Nebuchadnezzar II reportedly built an aboveground garden along the Euphrates River (near present-day Baghdad, Iraq) to grow exotic plants for his wife. Babylonian history never mentions the gardens, prompting some modern scholars to wonder if they ever existed.

The Statue of Zeus in Olympia was a 40-foot-tall seated statue of Zeus made of ivory and gold, built for his temple around 440 BCE. About the imposing statue, Greek geographer Strabo remarked, "If Zeus moved to stand up he would unroof the temple."[10] Fire destroyed it in 462 CE.

Mausoleum of Mausolus. Mausolus was a wealthy governor in Persia when he died in 352 BCE. His wife Artemisia built a 135-foot-tall, intricately sculptured tomb for him in Halicarnassus (present-day Bodrum, Turkey). The mausoleum fell during an earthquake in the 1300s CE.

Colossus of Rhodes. In 304 BCE, the people of Rhodes built a 100-foot-tall bronze statue of the city's patron god, Helios. The Colossus stood in the harbor for only 56 years, collapsing when its knees broke during an earthquake around 227 BCE. Pliny the Elder wrote of its size: "Few people can make their arms meet round the thumb."[11]

The Lighthouse of Alexandria, completed around 270 BCE, was the world's first lighthouse. To magnify light from a fire at the base, polished bronze mirrors were arranged at precise intervals inside the 380-foot-tall tower. The reflected light could be seen 35 miles away. The lighthouse became unusable after several earthquakes damaged it in the 1300s CE.

The Judgment of Paris, painted by Peter Paul Rubens in the 1630s, depicts a mythological beauty contest between Hera (right), Athena (left), and Aphrodite (middle). According to myth, each goddess bribed the judge, the mortal Paris (seated), to win his favor. Paris hands the golden apple trophy to Aphrodite when she promises him the love of the most beautiful woman in the world—King Menelaus' wife, Helen. The resulting jealousy among the goddesses, and of Menelaus, would lead to the Trojan War.

ARTEMIS

CHAPTER 3

The Protector of Women

Women needed all the help they could get, because ancient Greece was a man's world. While men participated in democratic government and thriving science and art communities, a typical adult woman spent her life shackled to her husband's household, or *Oikos* (OY-kohs). Unless she was extremely poor and had to work outside the home, a woman could not leave the house for fear of being seen, and coveted, by other men. In Athens, women were not allowed to vote or even go to school. In Athens' rival city of Sparta, women were allowed to vote, but little else.

All women were expected to marry as soon as they were biologically able to have children (at around fourteen years old). Older men, usually in their thirties, would claim them. Marriage was an important rite of passage for girls because it prepared them for motherhood. Producing healthy male babies was seen as the most important thing a woman could do in life because a male heir ensured the *Oikos* would continue. As women performed their reproductive duty, they hoped that Artemis would watch over them, just as she had her with own mother.

The Birth of Twin Olympians

That Zeus was a famous ladies' man was a constant source of frustration for his jealous wife, Hera. One of his many affairs was with the goddess Leto, known for her slender waist and long, flowing hair. Their romance was still young when she became pregnant with twins. Hera soon found out and, enraged, concocted a devious set of obstacles to prevent Leto from having the babies. First, Hera cursed Leto, forbidding her from giving birth anywhere on any solid ground.

In an engraving by sixteenth-century Italian printmaker Diana Scultori, Olympus' goddesses help Leto (center, lying down) and her twins recover after their famous birth on the rocky island of Delos.

Then she kidnapped Eileithyia (eyl-EYTH-ee-EYE-uh), the goddess of childbirth. If Eileithyia was not at Leto's side, Leto's babies could not be born. To finish the job, Hera also sent a monstrous snake to chase Leto and kill her before she could give birth.

Zeus saw what Hera was up to and sent the wind to take Leto to Poseidon, where she hid from the snake. Poseidon also knew of a floating island hidden under the water that was not covered by Hera's curse, and he raised it above the waves. This island, called Delos (DEE-lohs), was a barren and rocky place, but Leto promised great fame to Delos if it would keep her safe.

Even without Eileithyia, Leto quickly and painlessly gave birth to Artemis. Some sources say Artemis was born on Delos, but others suggest she was born on the neighboring island of Ortygia (or-TIH-jee-uh). Artemis then helped her mother across the sea so that Apollo could be born on Delos. All the most ancient and powerful goddesses except Hera came to witness the birth of Artemis' twin brother, Apollo. Artemis helped Leto as she labored with Apollo for nine days and nights, but Leto couldn't birth Apollo until Eileithyia arrived. The elder goddesses bribed the messenger goddess Iris, promising her a beautiful golden necklace if she would fetch Eileithyia from Hera's side. She did, and Apollo was born as soon as Eileithyia set foot on Delos. Leto kept her word, and Delos became famous for its temples to Leto's twins.

Artemis and Girlhood

As a young girl of three, Artemis sat in Zeus' lap and asked him to grant her three wishes. First, she said, "I want to be a virgin forever, Papa." Her second wish was for hunting equipment. "Please, Papa," she asked, "give me a bow and some arrows—please!—not a big fancy set: the Cyclopes can make me some slender arrows and a little, curved bow." She also asked Zeus to give her a group of young maidens, daughters of the Oceans and Forests—these would become her nymphs—to care for her hunting dogs. For her final wish, she asked him for claim to her favorite playground, the countryside. "Give me all the mountains in the world, Papa, and any old town, I don't care which one: Artemis will hardly ever go down into town. I'll live in the mountains, and visit men's cities only when women, struck with fierce labor pangs, call on my name."[1] Zeus was so amused by little Artemis that he granted her all her wishes.

Though she was a goddess of childbirth, perhaps her most important characteristic was her virginity. When Artemis requested that she should never have to marry, the goddess chose a life mortal women in ancient Greece could not. Artemis made it clear that she preferred the solitude of the hunt and the countryside to traditional, expected relationships with men. As feminist Susan Guettel Cole suggests, perhaps the Greeks thought Artemis "could protect girls, brides, and adult women from the dangers of reproduction only if she herself were immune to its disabilities."[2]

Artemis acted with her brother Apollo to watch over children. Niobe's myth illustrates that brother and sister used their arrows against people as well as animals, and it was said that they were responsible for sickness and death, especially in children. Boys who

fell suddenly ill and died were said to have been struck by Apollo's arrows; if a girl was afflicted, then Artemis was to blame. On the other hand, it was believed that Apollo and Artemis protected the children of loyal worshipers, so there was much to be gained by honoring the twin Olympians.

A well-known rite that celebrated Artemis' protection of young girls occurred at her temple in Brauron (BROW-ron), a small town in Attica. The annual Brauronia festival featured a goat sacrifice and the dance of the *arkterai* (ARK-tur-eye), or "little bears." The *arkterai* had their origins in myth, which told of a wild bear that lived around Brauron. One day a young girl teased the bear and, though it was usually tame, the bear lashed out and scratched the girl's face. In revenge, her brothers killed it, not knowing the bear was sacred to Artemis. The vengeful goddess sent a horrible plague to Brauron that would only be lifted when the town's young girls, pretending to be little bears, performed ritual dances for the goddess.

Honoring Artemis this way became a rite of passage for young girls in ancient Greece. As Libanius, a Roman scholar, put it, "Girls were required to serve Artemis before proceeding to the service of Aphrodite."[3] All Athenian girls between eight and thirteen years old were sent to Artemis' temple at Brauron. During their stay they were known as *arkterai* in reference to the myth, and dressed in robes dyed with saffron, a golden-yellow herb, to mimic bearskin. When a "little bear" reached puberty—a marriageable age—it was time for her to leave. Before leaving the temple, the "little bear" gathered all her childhood toys and dedicated them to Artemis. In doing this, she thanked the goddess for protecting her through her childhood and, at the same time, asked the goddess to bless her through the new challenges brought by childbirth. The girl's service complete, she was then free to marry. She had to leave Artemis' sanctuary in the countryside for a life in her husband's *Oikos* in the city. Artemis' chastity left no room in her temples for followers who had known romantic love.

Childbirth in Ancient Greece

Hippocrates, Father of
Modern Medicine

Artemis was very popular as the goddess of childbirth, and for good reason. In ancient Greece, pregnancy and childbirth were frequently fatal for mother, baby, or both. Any woman giving birth in ancient Greece (or anytime before the late nineteenth century CE—before the introduction of antiseptics and antibiotics) risked dying from disease, bleeding, or because the baby was too large to be born. In his *Epidemics*, the famous Greek doctor Hippocrates (hih-PAH-kruh-teez) noted 39 cases of childbirth-related health problems. Of these, nine women died.[4] Euripides' heroine Medea probably spoke for all Greek women when she said, "I would rather stand three times in the front of battle than bear one child."[5]

Pregnancy itself was a killer. During pregnancy, a woman's ability to fight off infection naturally diminishes. In ancient Greece, tuberculosis, malaria, and other fevers threatened the health of pregnant women and their unborn children. Also, healthy teen brides were practically required by society to become young mothers before their reproductive systems were fully mature. For teenagers, pregnancy and birth were more difficult, with lower survival rates, than for older women.[6]

Despite the challenges, the women of ancient Greece successfully delivered babies and survived more often than not. Deliveries took place in the woman's *oikos* and were attended by a midwife, assisted by a younger female or slave. Sometimes even the woman's father would attend the birth. A male doctor would be called in complicated cases, but there was usually little he could do. If he did intervene by, for example, placing herbal medicines in the womb, he was more likely to introduce infection.

Regardless of her fate, a woman gained socially from pregnancy and birth. If she lived, she enjoyed higher status in her *oikos* because she had done her part to continue the family line. If she died, she was considered a hero for having performed her duty to the community.

Renaissance painters were fascinated by Greek mythology. Renaissance master Titian painted *Diana and Callisto* for King Philip II of Spain. Diana (Artemis) points accusingly at Callisto, whose pregnant belly is revealed as other nymphs pull off her robes. Titian painted a partner canvas that shows Actaeon stumbling across a naked Artemis in the wilderness. The myth illustrates how lives can quickly be ruined by accidents and lies.

ARTEMIS

CHAPTER 4

The Goddess of Boundaries

Artemis asked Zeus for domain over the countryside because that was where her passion for the hunt kept her. The hunt was her only passion, and an odd one for a woman. Society required that mortal women focus all their attention on marriage, because the product of marriage—children—ensured that society would continue. Artemis' unwillingness to marry, and her firm demand to remain a virgin eternally, set her at odds with ancient Greek civilization. As modern historian Judith Barringer points out, the "Greeks regarded the female virgin as a type of wild animal, which could only be tamed through marriage."[1] It is interesting that Artemis is also the goddess of wild animals—apparently she was seen as one herself.

To protect her way of life from romantic love, Artemis set up boundaries between herself and society. She did this physically by living in the wilderness, but also emotionally by refusing love. Her followers obeyed the same strict rules, and all Greeks respected the boundaries of Artemis and her cult. Remembering that Artemis is a product of the ancient Greek culture, it's helpful to know that Greek audiences enjoyed hearing how these boundaries could be tested, so storytellers often placed the chaste Artemis or her followers in situations where romance could bloom. Violations of the boundaries were severely punished, as with Actaeon (Chapter 1). But as we see in the stories of Hippolytus (hih-PAH-lih-tus) and Callisto (kah-LIS-toh), when mortals put up their own boundaries through vows of chastity, they suffer unintended consequences.

Hippolytus' body, broken by his father's rage, is captured by sculptor Jean-Baptiste Lemoyne in *The Death of Hippolytus* (1715).

Hippolytus

Hippolytus was the son of Theseus, king of Athens, and Hippolyte, an Amazon queen. Swayed by Aphrodite's influence, Theseus had forced himself upon Hippolyte, and it was well known that Hippolytus was born from a union of violence. Hippolyte rejected

her son, because Amazons do not raise male children, so Hippolytus lived with his father. When he learned the story of his birth, Hippolytus was disgusted with his father and scorned Aphrodite. He became a devoted follower of Artemis and pledged to live a life of chastity.

Aphrodite thought Hippolytus was too proud and schemed to teach him a terrible lesson. When Theseus married Phaedra, Aphrodite made the young queen fall in love with her stepson. Phaedra burned with such passion that she couldn't keep her feelings inside. She told her nurse her secret, then asked her to tell Hippolytus, hoping that he would be interested, too. Chaste Hippolytus had sworn off women entirely and rejected his stepmother's advances, but swore to the nurse that he would keep his stepmother's scandalous feelings a secret. Phaedra was devastated. To make sure Hippolytus suffered for her as she had for him, Phaedra hanged herself and left a suicide note saying that Hippolytus had desired her and she couldn't live with the shame.

Theseus had never trusted his son. "What kind of man would want to be chaste?" he thought. When he read Phaedra's note, he believed her at once, thinking that Hippolytus' vow of chastity had covered up a sick desire for his wife. Theseus banished his son and called upon Poseidon, who had given the king three wishes. Theseus used one to wish for his son's death. Poseidon granted it.

As Hippolytus drove off in his chariot along the shore, an enormous wave appeared out of nowhere in the shape of a raging bull. The sea monster charged Hippolytus' chariot. His horses reared and tugged and pulled at the reins, and Hippolytus became entangled. The horses madly dashed to get away, dragging Hippolytus' body along the rocky coast. When Theseus heard what had happened, he instantly regretted his decision and called for his son's mangled body to be brought to him. According to

Euripides, Artemis herself visited her loyal follower on his deathbed. She told Theseus the awful truth of Phaedra's deception, and father and son were reconciled as Hippolytus took his last breath.

Callisto

Callisto, whose name means "most beautiful," was the daughter of Lycaon (ly-KAY-on), king of Arcadia. This Arcadian princess swore to remain a virgin forever and dedicated her life to Artemis, becoming the goddess's favorite nymph. But Zeus had seen Callisto's beauty and fell deeply in love with her. He knew an affair with Callisto would anger Hera, but as he leered at the girl from the heavens, he felt she would be worth the trouble.

One day, tired from a long hunt, Callisto rested alone in the woods. Zeus saw his opportunity and approached her, disguising himself as Artemis. "Girl," said Zeus through his disguise, "where have you been hunting within these woodlands that are my domain?" Callisto immediately rose from her nap and ran to hug her friend. "Greetings, goddess greater than Zeus: I say it even though he himself hears it!"[2] Zeus laughed and kissed her wildly, showing himself through his disguise. Callisto certainly did not expect that and fought against his romantic advances, but she was no match for the king of the gods. Pleased with himself, Zeus returned to Olympus, leaving Callisto ashamed and alone.

Artemis arrived in the grove before Callisto could fully recover from Zeus' attack. At first Callisto was wary and unsure, having just been tricked into thinking Artemis was there when she was not. But then Callisto saw all the nymphs surrounding the goddess and knew she was with her friends. Despite the welcome company, she blushed fiercely from the secret she would have to keep. She did not yet know that her secret would soon come to light—she was pregnant with Zeus' child.

Before Zeus' deception, Callisto enjoyed Artemis' favor. In *Diana Resting After Her Bath*, painted by François Boucher in 1742, Callisto waits on her sitting mistress, fresh kill from their hunt lying nearby. Artemis appears unguarded and attentive to her friend, unlike her haughty, accusing pose in Titian's depiction of Callisto (page 28).

For nine months, Callisto roamed the mountains with Artemis, hiding her growing belly beneath flowing robes. Callisto was heavy with child when, after a long day of hunting under the hot sun, Artemis asked her nymphs to join her for a bath. Callisto tried to excuse herself, but the goddess insisted. Callisto cried as she undressed and revealed to her goddess friend the result of her unwanted affair with Zeus. Artemis was furious at her friend's betrayal, even though Callisto was not at fault. Artemis screamed, "Go, far away from here: do not pollute

the sacred fountain!"[3] Callisto had no choice. She had to leave her mistress and her life behind.

Callisto soon gave birth to a baby boy, naming him Arcas (AR-kus) after her hometown. Hera saw everything from Olympus and seethed with rage that this child would be a constant reminder of Zeus' infidelity. The jealous wife cursed Callisto, saying, "Now, insolent girl, I will take that shape away from you, that pleased you and my husband so much!"[4] With that, beautiful Callisto turned into an ugly black bear with coarse fur and huge claws. Now she who was once the hunter became the hunted, and ran for her life from dogs and men with spears. Callisto roamed the forests, miserable and moaning, roaring loudly that Zeus had ruined her life and did not once come to her aid.

In the meantime, a nearby family adopted Arcas, and the boy never knew who his true parents were. At fifteen years old, when he went hunting, he encountered a black bear in the woods that stopped and looked at him in a strange way. It was Callisto. Though she had not seen Arcas since he was a baby, she recognized her son. She tried to scream his name but all that came out was a ferocious growl. Arcas had no idea who the bear really was, and he reached for his spear to defend himself. Seeing that the son was about to kill his mother, Zeus finally stepped in. Before anything happened, Zeus scooped up mother and son and turned them into stars, placing them in the sky together as the constellations Ursa Major (Great Bear) and Ursa Minor (Little Bear).

In these myths, both Hippolytus and Callisto are loyal to Artemis in spirit, but they suffer because Artemis' boundary of chastity is difficult to keep in a world where the temptation of romantic love exists. The boundaries that work for Artemis, because she is a goddess, only cause trouble for mere mortals.

Constellations

Ancient Greeks used myths to explain how constellations—groups of stars that form a recognizable shape—arrived in the sky. Around 150 CE, the astronomer Ptolemy published his *Almagest* (Arabic for "Great Book"), which grouped 1,022 stars into 48 constellations. This book was considered the authority on astronomy in Europe for almost 1,500 years. Even in modern times, astronomers divide the sky using Ptolemy's constellations in the Northern Hemisphere. They add another 40 from the Southern Hemisphere that the Greeks could not have seen.

Artemis set Callisto in the sky as Ursa Major, Latin for "larger bear."

Artemis is involved in the creation of three well-known constellations—Ursa Major (the Great Bear), Ursa Minor (the Little Bear), and Orion (the Hunter). All civilizations that have written records, from Native Americans to the ancient Chinese, have recorded some kind of myth about each of them.

According to Greek myth, Ursa Major represents Artemis' hunting companion Callisto, who was turned into a bear and reunited in the sky with her son, Arcas (Ursa Minor). In North America, Ursa Major and Ursa Minor are more commonly known as the Big Dipper and Little Dipper, respectively. To the Greeks, the bowl of the dipper was the bear's body, with the dipper's handle as the tail. Ursa Minor's handle contains the North Star, Polaris, which guided many ancient peoples at sea.

Orion is one of the largest constellations in the sky, befitting its namesake, who was a giant hunter. Bright stars pinpoint Orion's head, shoulders, and knees. Even as a star formation, Orion is ready for the hunt. A sword of stars seems to hang from a "belt" made of three evenly spaced stars. Next to Orion are his two hunting dogs, the constellations Canis Major and Canis Minor, and nearby are two wild animals—Lepus the Hare and Taurus the Bull—to hunt for eternity.

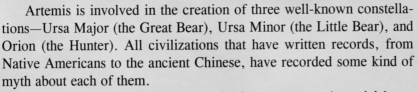

The statue Aphrodite of Soli, found at a temple to Aphrodite in Soli on Cyprus. As the goddess of romantic love, the beautiful and passionate Aphrodite was Artemis' polar opposite. According to myth, she was not born, but rose fully grown from foam in the sea near the island of Cyprus.

ARTEMIS

CHAPTER 5

The Hunter Becomes
the Hunted

Artemis is perhaps best known as goddess of the hunt because of the wealth of artwork, both ancient and modern, showing her in the act of hunting. The hunt in ancient Greece was a peaceful sport for men rich enough to have free time. It is interesting then that Artemis, a woman, rules over hunting, when ancient Greeks would never have allowed women to hunt. However, in Greek mythology, the hunt was a metaphor for romance, where a man, a "hunter," pursued his ultimate trophy, a beautiful wife. Myths are full of destructive romantic entanglements, and these all begin when Aphrodite's archer son Eros (known as Cupid to the Romans) hunts a lover, shooting him or her with a magic arrow. Only the virgin goddesses Athena, Hestia, and Artemis escaped Aphrodite's power over love. Whereas Aphrodite represents pure passion, completely lacking self-control, Artemis is her opposite, and her self-control is her prized possession. It is important, then, that Artemis is the hunting goddess, because she represents the woman who can never be caught.

Orion (oh-RY-un) was a "hunter" of women, and, though his myth has many versions, all spell death for him once he encounters Artemis.

Orion

Orion was a legendary hunter, a giant, and Poseidon's son. In one version of Orion's myth, Orion fell in love with Merope (MEHR-uh-pee), the daughter of King Oenopion (ee-NOH-pee-on) of the island of Chios (KY-ohs). The king hated Orion, having heard that Orion had forced himself on Merope while she slept. One night the king invited Orion to dinner in his castle, all the while slipping the hunter

In *The Blind Orion Searching for the Rising Sun* (detail) by Nicolas Poussin (1658), Orion is guided toward Eos while Artemis looks on from a cloud.

glass after glass of wine. When Orion was sufficiently drunk, the king attacked him, put out his eyes, and had the castle guards toss him on the beach to die.

The next morning, Eos (EE-ohs), the goddess of dawn, saw Orion and took pity on him, giving him back his sight. Orion knew he had to prove himself so that Merope's father would let them marry. The great warrior offered to hunt and kill all the wild beasts on the island. Oenopion accepted, reluctantly impressed that Orion would return after the king had left him for dead.

As Orion wandered the island, he met Artemis in the wilderness. The goddess was so beautiful that he instantly forgot all about Merope and fell in love with Artemis instead. As he moved to kiss her, Artemis turned the dust at his feet into a scorpion that stung him to death. Once she had taught him this ultimate lesson, she turned his body into stars and set them in the sky. She also placed the constellation Scorpio, the scorpion, behind Orion to keep him on the run for eternity.

Other versions of Orion's story say he and Artemis were dear friends and hunting companions. Their closeness enraged Apollo, who thought his sister's chastity might be in danger. One day at the seashore together, Apollo set out to trick the lovers. When Artemis wasn't watching, Apollo, who knew Orion was proud of his strength, challenged the hunter to swim far away from the beach. Apollo watched Orion swim so far out that he became a speck on the horizon. Apollo called Artemis over, a different challenge in mind for her.

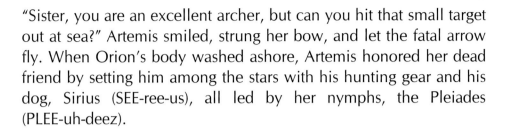
"Sister, you are an excellent archer, but can you hit that small target out at sea?" Artemis smiled, strung her bow, and let the fatal arrow fly. When Orion's body washed ashore, Artemis honored her dead friend by setting him among the stars with his hunting gear and his dog, Sirius (SEE-ree-us), all led by her nymphs, the Pleiades (PLEE-uh-deez).

Calydonian Boar

The story of the Calydonian boar featured perhaps the most exciting hunt of its time. This myth begins as yet another tale of Artemis' revenge on a mortal, but the real focus of the story is on the forbidden romance between a prince, Meleager (meh-lee-AY-gur), and an Amazon warrior, Atalanta (aa-tuh-LAN-tuh). The romantic aspect of the chase was so important to the Greeks that this story was featured prominently in artwork on wedding vases.

King Oeneus (EE-nee-us) ruled Calydon (KAA-luh-dun) in Aetolia (ee-TOH-lee-uh). The fertile land there always yielded a rich harvest, and each year, the pious Oeneus offered the first of the crop to the gods in thanks. But one year Oeneus forgot to include Artemis in his sacrifice. The goddess was furious at his neglect. To punish him, she sent an enormous monster, a wild boar, to Calydon.

The boar ran through the fields, trampling the crops and attacking and killing the livestock, fittingly taking away that which Oeneus forgot to give Artemis. The people of Calydon ran for their lives to the safety of their walled city. From within, they could only watch helplessly as the boar ruined their harvest and threatened them with starvation. King Oeneus' son Meleager left the city to get help, returning with a crowd of famous heroes eager to battle this fierce beast.

Among the crowd of brave men was a woman named Atalanta, who was a favorite of Artemis. When Atalanta was born, her father abandoned her in the forest to die, but she lived because Artemis sent a mother bear to take care of her. As a young woman, Atalanta became a skilled hunter and was eventually adopted by the Amazon tribe as one of its own. Atalanta proved that she was strong and fierce as well as beautiful. As they hunted together, Meleager fell in love with Atalanta.

The warriors and their hounds chased the boar through the countryside surrounding Calydon. The warriors did their best to attack the beast with spears, axes, and arrows, but Artemis' unseen hand protected the boar from their blows. Several young men lost their lives to the boar's sharp tusks. After a long and one-sided battle, Atalanta landed an arrow behind the boar's ear, bloodying its head and back. With the beast slowed somewhat, Meleager threw his spear into the boar's back, fatally wounding it.

The warriors all cheered for Meleager and gathered around the dead boar. Artemis was not pleased. As she looked down on the scene from Mount Olympus, she set them to arguing over the prize. Remembering how his new love took the boar's first blood, Meleager held out the boar's head and skin and said to Atalanta, "Take the prize that is mine by right, and let my glory be shared with you."[1] Atalanta was pleased, but the other hunters were shocked that Meleager would give such a magnificent trophy to a woman. Meleager's uncles Toxeus (TOK-see-us) and Plexippus (PLEK-sih-pus) thought such a handsome prize should stay in the family. They snatched it from her, saying, "Those rightly belong to us and not the likes of you, woman." Meleager was outraged at this insult to Atlanta and drew his sword once more, killing his uncles on the spot.

News of the deaths of Toxeus and Plexippus quickly reached Meleager's mother, Althaea (al-THAY-uh). Her brothers had been dear to her and she decided that her son should pay with his life. Unfortunately, his life was in her power to take. When Meleager was born, the Fates foretold that he would die once an enchanted twig in King Oeneus' fireplace was burned. Naturally, Althaea hid the twig to ensure a long life for her son. But with her brothers dead by Meleager's hand, she fetched the twig and burned it. Meleager

A carving on an alabaster ash urn found in Volterra, Italy, shows Meleager and Atalanta working together to kill the Calydonian boar.

died immediately, giving Artemis her ultimate revenge against King Oeneus.

In the Calydonian boar myth, the obvious punishment is against Oeneus, who forgot to honor Artemis. His crops are destroyed and, in the end, is son is dead. But Meleager is also punished because he fell in love with the wrong woman. As an Amazon, Atalanta stood outside society, like a priestess to Artemis. She was even raised by a bear. Meleager could never actually "catch" Atalanta, but he was blinded by his love for her. His passion made him out of control and, through his actions, caused his death.

As a hunter, virgin, and protector of women, all at the same time, the goddess Artemis reflected the ideals of the society that created her. Some modern historians have seen her as one of the first feminists. She made her own rules and lived outside the society men had created. On the other hand, her isolation caused problems for everybody else who had to live in the man's world of ancient Greece. Her mortal followers were inevitably confronted with romantic love, and it led to their downfall. Even non-followers had to respect Artemis' boundaries or they would pay with their lives. As much as Artemis tried to be her own woman, the society of ancient Greece ensured she would be just that—alone.

Amazon Warrior Women

According to myth, the Amazons were a tribe of warrior women descended from Ares, the god of war. Legend has it that the word Amazon derives from the Greek *a-*, "without," and *mazos*, "breast," because the warrior women were rumored to cut off one of their breasts to more efficiently handle a bow. In the *Iliad*, Homer says that Amazons continued their society by mating with male warriors before killing them. The Amazons raised

Amazon warrior women

any female offspring resulting from these unions, whereas boy babies were either killed or abandoned. Greece was a male-centered society, and so, according to modern historian Judith Barringer, myth writers used stories of the Amazons to "offer a negative image of what might happen if women were in control, or provide a model of women who refuse marriage and, therefore, refuse culture."[2] Not surprisingly, the Amazons were devoted worshipers of Artemis.

But were the Amazons more than myth? Herodotus wrote that they actually existed, as a group of women warriors who lost to the Greeks at the battle of Thermodon. They were put to work on Greek ships as slaves, but successfully mutinied, killing their captors and taking control. The Amazons drifted to the shore of the Black Sea and joined the Scythian culture there. Over time, the Amazons and Scythians moved northeast to the Russian steppes, where they became the Sauromatian culture.

Following Herodotus, archaeologist Jeannine Davis-Kimball examined Sauromatian burial sites. She found skeletons of women buried with weapons and bone injuries that could only have come from battle. Leg bones of female skeletons were bowed, showing a life spent mostly on horseback. Davis-Kimball says that these findings are probably not unique to the Sauromatians, but that Amazon-type warriors were quite common: "Our new evidence shows that women have always had a pretty prominent place in nomadic societies."[3] Using DNA samples from the skeletons, Davis-Kimball also showed that modern-day Mongolians descended from Herodotus' Amazon women.

Chapter 1. The Virgin Goddess and Her Sacred Deer

1. Ovid, *Metamorphoses*, translated by A.S. Kline, http://www.tonykline.co.uk/PITBR/Latin/Ovhome.htm, Book III, lines 165–205.

2. Mark Waid, *The Origin of Wonder Woman*, DC Comics, http://www.dccomics.com/sites/52/?action

3. Ibid.

4. Garland Voss, "The Saga of Wonder Woman," *Starforce*, July 1978, http://www.wonderwoman-online.com/articles/starforce.html

Chapter 2. Religious with a Vengeance

1. Susan Guettel Cole, "Domesticating Artemis." *The Sacred and the Feminine in Ancient Greece*, edited by Sue Blundell and Margaret Williamson (London: Routledge, 1998), p. 31.

2. Ovid, *Metamorphoses*, translated by A.S. Kline, http://www.tonykline.co.uk/PITBR/Latin/Ovhome.htm, Book VI, lines 267–312.

3. Euripides, *Iphigenia at Aulis*, translated by E. P. Coleridge, http://etext.library.adelaide.edu.au/e/euripides/ip_aulis/, line 1395.

4. Ibid., line 1555.

5. Lee Krystek, "The Temple of Artemis," The UnMuseum, http://www.unmuseum.org/ephesus.htm.

6. Plutarch, "The Life of Alexander," *The Parallel Lives*, translated by Bernadotte Perrin (Cambridge, Massachusetts: Harvard University Press, 1919), http://penelope.uchicago.edu/Thayer/E/Roman/Texts/Plutarch/Lives/Alexander*/3.html#3.5, Book III, verse 5.

7. British Museum, "The Later Temple of Artemis at Ephesos," n.d., http://www.thebritishmuseum.ac.uk/explore/highlights/article_index/l/the_later_temple_of_artemis_at.aspx

8. The Holy Bible, King James Version, Acts 19: 24-28.

9. Alaa K. Ashmawy, *The Seven Wonders of the Ancient World*, "Great Pyramid of Giza," http://ce.eng.usf.edu/pharos/wonders/pyramid.html

10. Alaa K. Ashmawy, *The Seven Wonders of the Ancient World*, "The Statue of Zeus at Olympia," http://ce.eng.usf.edu/pharos/wonders/zeus.html

11. Alaa K. Ashmawy, *The Seven Wonders of the Ancient World*, "The Colossus of Rhodes," http://ce.eng.usf.edu/pharos/wonders/colossus.html

Chapter 3. The Protector of Women

1. Callimachus, *Hymns 1–3*, "Hymn to Artemis," translated by A.W. Mair and G. R. Mair (Cambridge, Massachusetts: Harvard University Press, 1921), verse 3.

2. Susan Guettel Cole, "Domesticating Artemis," *The Sacred and the Feminine in Ancient Greece*, edited by Sue Blundell and Margaret Williamson (London: Routledge, 1998), p. 32.

3. Ibid.

4. Nancy Demand, *Birth, Death, and Motherhood in Classical Greece* (Baltimore: The Johns Hopkins University Press, 1994), pp. 48–55.

5. Euripides, Euripides 1, *The Complete Greek Tragedies, The Medea*, translated by Rex Warner (New York: Washington Square Press, 1968), p. 72.

6. Demand, pp. 123–126.

Chapter 4. The Goddess of Boundaries

1. Judith Barringer, *The Hunt in Ancient Greece* (Baltimore: The Johns Hopkins University Press, 2001), p. 170.

2. Ovid, *Metamorphoses*, translated by A.S. Kline, http://www.tonykline.co.uk/PITBR/Latin/Ovhome.htm. Book II, verses 417–440.

3. Ibid., verses 441–465.

4. Ibid., verses 466–495.

Chapter 5. The Hunter Becomes the Hunted

1. Ovid, *Metamorphoses*, translated by A.S. Kline, http://www.tonykline.co.uk/PITBR/Latin/Ovhome.htm, Book VIII, verses 425–450.

2. Judith Barringer, *The Hunt in Ancient Greece* (Baltimore: The Johns Hopkins University Press, 2001), p. 157.

3. Kathy Svitil, "Interview with Jeannine Davis-Kimball," *Secrets of the Dead: Amazon Warrior Women*, 2004, http://www.pbs.org/wnet/secrets/case_amazon/interview.html

FURTHER READING

For Young Adults

D'Aulaire, Ingri, and Edgar Parin D'Aulaire. *D'Aulaires' Book of Greek Myths*. New York: Delacorte Books for Young Readers, 1992.

Evslin, Bernard. *Greek Gods*. New York: Scholastic, Inc., 1995.

——. *Heroes, Gods, and Monsters of Greek Myths*. New York: Random House, 1984.

Macdonald, Fiona. *Gods and Goddesses in the Daily Life of the Ancient Greeks*. Columbus, Ohio: Peter Bedrick Books, 2002.

——. *I Wonder Why Greeks Built Temples and Other Questions About Ancient Greece*. New York: Kingfisher, 2006.

——. *Women in Ancient Greece*. New York: Peter Bedrick Books, 1999.

FURTHER READING

Works Consulted

Adkins, Lesley, and Roy A. Adkins. *Handbook to Life in Ancient Greece*. New York: Facts on File, Inc., 2005.

Apollodorus. *The Library*. Translated by Sir James George Frazer. Cambridge, Massachusetts: Harvard University Press, 1921. http://www.theoi.com/Text/ApollodorusE.html

Ashmawy, Alaa K. *The Seven Wonders of the Ancient World*. http://ce.eng.usf.edu/pharos/wonders/index.html.

Barringer, Judith M. *The Hunt in Ancient Greece*. Baltimore:The Johns HopkinsUniversity Press, 2001.

Bell, Cathy. *The Mythology of the Constellations*. http://www.comfychair.org/ ~ cmbell/myth/myth.html

British Museum. "The Later Temple of Artemis at Ephesos." http://www.thebritishmuseum.ac.uk/explore/highlights/article_index/l/the_later_temple_of_artemis_at.aspx

Callimachus. *Hymns and Epigrams*. Lycophron. Aratus. Translated by A. W. Mair and G. R. Mair. Cambridge, Massachusetts: Harvard University Press, 1921. http://www.theoi.com/Text/CallimachusHymns1.html

Demand, Nancy. *Birth, Death, and Motherhood in Classical Greece*. Baltimore: The Johns Hopkins University Press, 1994.

Dowden, Ken. *The Uses of Greek Mythology*. London: Routledge, 1992.

Downing, Christine. *The Goddess*. New York: The Crossroad Publishing Company, 1981.

Goff, Barbara. *Citizen Bacchae*. Berkeley: University of California Press, 2004.

Harrison, Jane Ellen. *Themis*. Cambridge, England: Cambridge University Press, 1912.

Hesiod. *Homeric Hymns, Epic Cycle, Homerica*. Translated by H.G. Evelyn-White. Cambridge, Massachusetts: Harvard University Press, 1914. http://www.theoi.com/Text/HomericHymns1.html

Homer. *The Iliad*. Translated by Samuel Butler. Edited by Louise R. Loomis. Roslyn, New York: Walter J. Black, Inc., 1942.

——. *The Odyssey*. Translated by Samuel Butler. Edited by Louise Ropes Loomis. Roslyn, New York: Walter J. Black, Inc., 1944.

Hyginus. *Hyginus Fabulae*. Translated and edited by Mary Grant. Lawrence: University of Kansas Press, 1960. http://www.theoi.com/Text/HyginusFabulae1.html

Lethaby, W. R. *Diana's Temple at Ancient Greece*. London: B.T. Batsford, 1908. http://penelope.uchicago.edu/Thayer/E/Gazetteer/Places/Europe/Turkey/_Periods/Greek/_Texts/LETGKB/Ephesus*.html

Lyons, Deborah. *Gender and Immortality*. Princeton, New Jersey: Princeton University Press, 1997.

Morford, Mark P. O., and Robert J. Lenardon. *Classical Mythology*. New York: Oxford University Press, 2003.

Ovid. *Metamorphoses*. Translated by A.S. Kline. http://www.tonykline.co.uk/PITBR/Latin/Ovhome.htm

Pedley, John. *Sanctuaries and the Sacred in the Ancient Greek World*. Cambridge, England: Cambridge University Press, 2005.

Plutarch. *The Parallel Lives*. Translated by Bernadotte Perrin. Cambridge, Massachusetts: Harvard University Press, 1914. http://penelope.uchicago.edu/Thayer/E/Roman/Texts/Plutarch/Lives/Alexander*/3.html

Richard, Olive. "Our Women Are Our Future," *Family Circle*, August 14, 1942, http://www.wonderwoman-online.com/articles/fc-marston.html

Rose, H. J. *Ancient Greek and Roman Religion*. New York: Barnes & Noble Books, 1995.

Svitil, Kathy. "Interview with Jeannine Davis-Kimball." *Secrets of the Dead: Amazon Warrior Women*, " 2004, http://www.pbs.org/wnet/secrets/case_amazon/interview.html

The Sacred and the Feminine in Ancient Greece. Edited by Sue Blundell and Margaret Williamson. London: Routledge, 1998.

Voss, Garland. "The Saga of Wonder Woman." *Starforce*, July 1978, http://www.wonderwoman-online.com/articles/starforce.html

Waid, Mark. *The Origin of Wonder Woman*. DC Comics, http://www.dccomics.com/sites/52/?action=biography&w=1

Women's Religions in the Greco-Roman World: A Sourcebook. Edited by Ross Shepard Kraemer. Oxford, England: Oxford University Press, 2004.

On the Internet
Ancient Greece: Projects and Internet Resources
    http://www.internet-at-work.com/hos_mcgrane/greece/eg_greece_intro.html
Constellation Mythology
    http://www.coldwater.k12.mi.us/lms/planetarium/myth/index.html
Daily Life in Ancient Greece
    http://members.aol.com/Donnclass/Greeklife.html

carcass (KAR-kus)—The body of a dead animal.

chastity (CHAA-stih-tee)—The quality of being modest; restraint in matters of love, especially because of religious beliefs. One who has chastity is chaste (CHAYST).

cult—A system of religious beliefs that includes worshiping a particular deity, place, or thing.

deity (DEE-ih-tee)—A god or goddess.

immortal (ih-MOR-tul)—A person who cannot die, such as a god.

mortal—Someone who will, one day, die, as opposed to an immortal.

nomadic (noh-MAA-dik)—In the manner of a person with no permanent home who moves from place to place, usually according to the season.

nymph (NIMF)—A beautiful maiden deity. Nymphs are associated with natural objects (such as trees or rivers), and usually act as servants to a higher-ranking god or goddess (such as Artemis).

plague (PLAYG)—A deadly disease that spreads easily.

polytheistic (pah-lee-thee-IS-tik)—Involving many gods.

prophecy (PRAH-feh-see)—A foretelling of an event, revealed by a prophet or seer.

retribution (reh-trih-BYOO-shun)—Something given as punishment.

syncretism (SIN-kreh-tism)—A merging of different religious beliefs. From the Greek *synkretismos*, "union of communities."

vengeful (VENJ-ful)—Desiring revenge.